GREEN LEARNING
ACADEMY

Countries and Cultures

# Peru

## by Allison Lassieur

**Content Consultant:**
Dr. Thomas Brown, Professor of Latin American History
Augustana College
Rock Island, Illinois

**Reading Consultant:**
Dr. Robert Miller, Professor of Special Populations
Minnesota State University, Mankato

Capstone press
Mankato, Minnesota

Capstone Press
151 Good Counsel Drive, P.O. Box 669, Mankato, MN 56002
http://www.capstone-press.com

Copyright © 2004 by Capstone Press. All rights reserved.
No part of this publication may be reproduced in whole or in part, or stored in a retrieval system, or transmitted in any form or by any means, electronic, mechanical, photocopying, recording, or otherwise, without written permission of the publisher. For information regarding permission, write to Capstone Press, 151 Good Counsel Drive, P.O. Box 669, Dept. R, Mankato, Minnesota 56002.
Printed in the United States of America

*Library of Congress Cataloging-in-Publication Data*
Lassieur, Allison.
   Peru / by Allison Lassieur.
   p. cm.—(Countries and cultures)
   Includes bibliographical references and index.
   ISBN 0-7368-2176-7 (Hardcover)
   1. Peru—Juvenile literature. I. Title. II. Series.
F3408.5.L37 2004
985—dc21                                                                               2003002651

Summary: Discusses the geography, history, economy, and people of Peru.

**Editorial Credits**
Gillia Olson, editor; Heather Kindseth, series designer; Molly Nei, book designer; Alta Schaffer, photo researcher; Karen Risch, product planning editor

**Photo Credits**
Cover photos: Machu Picchu, Tom Till; hand-woven Peruvian blankets, Michele Burgess

AP/Wide World Photos, 33; Archive Photos by Getty Images, 29; Blaine Harrington III, 36; Bruce Coleman, Inc./Tom Brakefield, 17; Bruce Coleman Inc./Hans Reinhard, 56; Capstone Press/Gary Sundermeyer, 53; Corbis/Bettmann, 25, 30; Corbis/Yann Arthus-Bertrand, 18; Cory Langley, 1 (all), 63; Doranne Jacobson, 50; Houserstock/Michael J. Pettypool, 35; James P. Rowan, 13; Michele Burgess, 11, 44; Mireille Vautier, 46, 49; North Wind Picture Archives, 21, 23, 26; One Mile Up Inc., 57 (both); Pete & Jill Yearneau, 43 (bills); Sally Gray, 4; TRIP/R. Bognar, 54; Victor Englebert, 8, 39

**Artistic Effects**
BrandXPictures, Corbis, Digital Stock, Digital Vision, Earthstar, PhotoDisc, Inc.

1 2 3 4 5 6     08 07 06 05 04 03

# Contents

## Chapter 1
Fast Facts about Peru ............................................................... 4
**Explore Peru** ......................................................................... 5

## Chapter 2
Fast Facts about Peru's Land ..................................................... 8
**Peru's Land, Climate, and Wildlife** ........................................... 9

## Chapter 3
Fast Facts about Peru's History ................................................ 18
**Peru's History and Government** ............................................. 19

## Chapter 4
Fast Facts about Peru's Economy .............................................. 36
**Peru's Economy** .................................................................. 37

## Chapter 5
Fast Facts about Peru's People .................................................. 44
**Peru's People, Culture, and Daily Life** .................................... 45

## Maps
Geopolitical Map of Peru .......................................................... 7
Peru's Land Regions and Topography ...................................... 15
Peru's Industries and Natural Resources .................................. 40

## Features
Giant River Otter ................................................................... 17
Peru's Money ........................................................................ 43
Learn to Speak Spanish ......................................................... 50
Recipe: Make Arroz Con Leche ............................................... 53
Peru's National Symbols ........................................................ 57
Timeline .............................................................................. 58
Words to Know ..................................................................... 60
To Learn More ...................................................................... 61
Useful Addresses .................................................................. 62
Internet Sites ....................................................................... 62
Index .................................................................................. 64

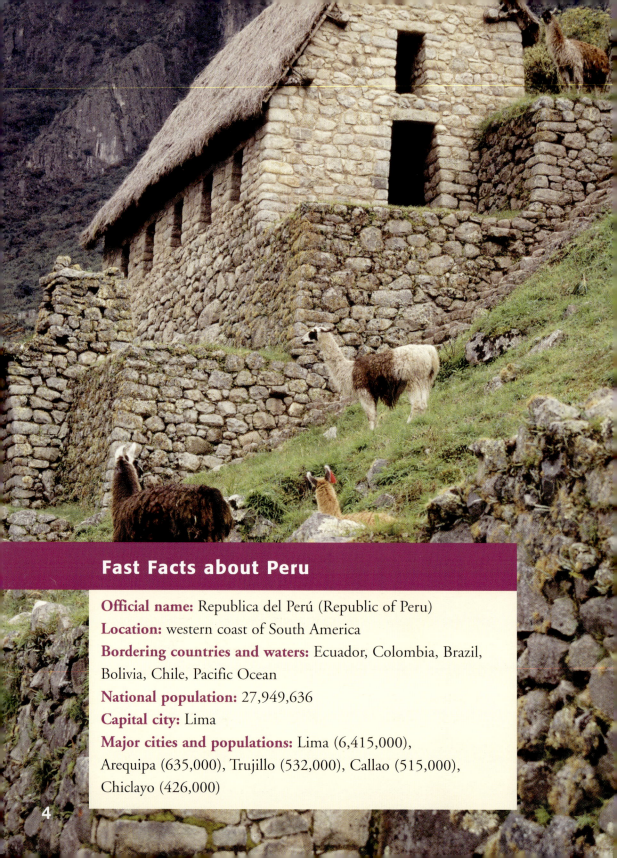

## Fast Facts about Peru

**Official name:** Republica del Perú (Republic of Peru)
**Location:** western coast of South America
**Bordering countries and waters:** Ecuador, Colombia, Brazil, Bolivia, Chile, Pacific Ocean
**National population:** 27,949,636
**Capital city:** Lima
**Major cities and populations:** Lima (6,415,000), Arequipa (635,000), Trujillo (532,000), Callao (515,000), Chiclayo (426,000)

# Chapter 1

# Explore Peru

Mysterious ruins lie deep in Peru's wilderness. The ruins of Machu Picchu make up one of the world's most famous archaeological sites. The site is hidden away between two mountain peaks about 50 miles (80 kilometers) northwest of Cuzco.

Machu Picchu is one of the most important surviving sites of the Inca civilization. The Inca built the city in the mid-1400s. They built strong stone houses and temples. They used raised dirt platforms, called terraces, for growing food. Some historians believe Inca royalty sometimes stayed in the city.

Machu Picchu was abandoned in the 1500s. Historians and archaeologists are unsure why the Inca left the city. Although local people knew of the site, people outside of Peru did not learn about it until 1911. In that year, American archaeologist Hiram Bingham visited the site. Today, archaeologists

◀ The Inca built strong stone houses and terraces at Machu Picchu. Today, llamas roam the site.

continue to study the site to learn about the Inca. About 300,000 tourists visit the site each year. Visitors travel over steep mountain pathways through dense rain forest to get there.

## Peru

Peru lies along the Pacific Ocean in northwestern South America. It borders Ecuador and Colombia on its northern edge. Brazil, Bolivia, and Chile border Peru on the east and south. Because of its location, Peru has sunny beaches, tall mountains, and steamy rain forests within its borders.

Peru is the third largest country in South America, covering 496,222 square miles (1,285,215 square kilometers). It is about three times the size of the U.S. state of California. Peru has a population of about 28 million people.

Peru's natural resources and rich culture give it a bright future. It is a leading producer of silver, copper, lead, and zinc. Peru's tourism industry continues to grow. Peruvians continue to develop the country's resources to improve their lives.

## Fast Facts about Peru's Land

**Area:** 496,222 square miles (1,285,215 square kilometers)
**Latitude and longitude:** 10 degrees south latitude, 76 degrees west longitude at Peru's geographic center
**Highest elevation:** Nevado Huascarán, 22,205 feet (6,768 meters)
**Lowest elevation:** Pacific Ocean, sea level

Chapter 2

# Peru's Land, Climate, and Wildlife

Peru is a land of great contrasts. Miles of flat, fertile Pacific coastland stretch the length of the country. Just east of the coast lie the snow-capped Andes Mountains. East of the Andes is the hot, humid rain forest region. Three regions, the coastal zone, the sierra, and the selva, divide Peru's landscape.

## The Coastal Zone

The coastal zone of Peru is a long, narrow region between the Pacific shore and the Andes Mountains. It is about 1,500 miles (2,400 kilometers) long, but it is only between 12 and 62 miles (19 to 100 kilometers) wide. It makes up only 10 percent of Peru's total land area. Most of the coastal area is rugged and dry. The Sechura Desert in northern Peru contains huge sand dunes.

◀ A green valley lies between sand dunes on Peru's dry coast. People farm near rivers where they can get water for crops.

Although the coastal zone is very dry, most of Peru's large cities, factories, and commercial farms are found there. Peru's capital, Lima, is located along the coast. More than 50 rivers cross the coastal region. They provide water for irrigation and drinking water in the cities. The broad valleys along the Ica and Chicama Rivers provide especially good farmland.

An interesting feature of Peru's coast is the fog. A thick, gray fog generally covers the entire coast from May to November. Peruvians call it the garua. It is famous for the mist and light rain that come with it. Small areas of the coast are always covered by heavy fog. The fog's moisture allows plants to grow in normally barren desert areas. Peruvians call these areas "lomas."

## The Sierra

Peru's sierra, or mountain, region covers almost one-third of the country's territory. The sierra region includes the Andes Mountains. The Andes Mountains are a series of ranges that run north and south just inland of the Pacific coast of South America. The Andes are called the backbone of South America.

Within Peru, the Andes are separated into several ranges. The Cordillera Occidental runs parallel to the coast. The Cordillera Central lies northeast of the Occidental. Even farther east lies the Cordillera

▲ Lake Titicaca is located in Peru's sierra region.

Oriental. Plateaus, canyons, and basins separate these ranges. Colca Canyon, one of the world's deepest canyons, lies in southern Peru.

A few areas of the sierra also have beautiful, glittering lakes. Lake Titicaca is located between Peru and Bolivia. Lake Titicaca lies at an elevation of 12,500 feet (3,810 meters). It is the highest lake in the world that is deep enough and wide enough to allow ships to sail on it.

## The Selva

Thick forests make up Peru's rain forest region. Peruvians call this region the selva. It is Peru's largest region, but only 11 percent of the country's people live there.

The selva can be divided into two subregions, the high selva and the low selva. The high selva includes the heavily forested foothills of the eastern Andes. The high selva slopes down eastward to the plains of the low selva. Thick rain forests cover most of the low selva.

A huge network of rivers crisscross the entire selva. Two of Peru's most important rivers, the Marañón River and the Ucayali River, flow through the low selva. They join the Amazon River in northern Peru, which eventually crosses the border into Brazil.

The selva region interests tourists and scientists. The area is popular with tourists who want to experience South American rain forests. Scientists work with rain forest plants to create new medicines. Scientists have already found uses for some rain forest plant life. The cinchona tree produces quinine, which is used to fight the disease malaria. Peru shows the cinchona tree on its coat of arms.

## Climate

Peru's location near the equator makes it a tropical country. However, an unusually cool ocean current,

▲ Rain forests grow in Peru's low selva.

called the Peru Current or Humboldt Current, makes the coast cool. The coastal climate is moderate all year, averaging about 68 degrees Fahrenheit (20 degrees Celsius).

Peru's climate, and that of many other countries, can be greatly affected by El Niño. This seasonal, warm ocean current flows along the equator in the Pacific Ocean. Sometimes, El Niño flows far south, partly or mostly replacing the Peru Current. Water

> **Did you know...?**
> El Niño means "the boy child" in Spanish. The name refers to Jesus. It has this name because it usually appears during the Christmas season, when Christians celebrate Jesus' birth.

temperatures off Peru's coast rise several degrees, causing climate change. Dry areas may be flooded from heavy rains, while wet areas experience droughts. Other ocean currents are affected, which affects climates throughout the world. El Niño is blamed for floods, droughts, and severe storms around the globe.

While temperatures in Peru's sierra region differ widely, temperatures in the selva remain fairly constant. The upper elevations of the sierra have permanent ice and snow cover. In the lower elevations, temperatures rarely dip below freezing. The selva rain forests stay warm and humid throughout most of the year. The temperature averages 80 degrees Fahrenheit (27 degrees Celsius).

Peru's rainfall gradually increases from west to east. Most of the coastal zone receives less than 2 inches (5 centimeters) of rain each year. The western side of the Andes receives little more than the coast. The eastern side of the Andes and the selva, however, often receive more than 80 inches (200 centimeters) of rain each year.

## Peru's Land Regions and Topography

**KEY**
- Coastal Zone
- Sierra
- Selva
- Desert
- Mountain
- Mountain Range
- River

## Wildlife

Most of Peru's wildlife is in the mountains and rain forests. Rain forests contain the most diverse plant and animal life in the world. Mahogany, cedar, and rubber trees grow there. Rain forest animals include the jaguar, the piglike peccary, many types of monkeys, and a great variety of snakes and insects. The anaconda, the world's largest snake, slithers through the rain forest. The world's largest rodent, the capybara, can grow to weigh 100 pounds (45 kilograms) in Peru's rain forest.

Many Peruvian animals are rare or endangered. The taruka, or Andean stag, is one of the rarest. Local villagers hunt this deerlike animal for food. Today, it survives only in the wildest areas of the Andes. One of the best-known endangered Peruvian animals is the Andean condor. It is the largest flying bird on Earth. Condors have a wingspan of up to 10 feet (3 meters). Besides Peru, condors live in other areas of the Andes.

Several species of lamoids are native to Peru. Lamoids are a group of mammals that include llamas, alpacas, and camels. Peruvians use llamas and alpacas to carry heavy loads. Alpacas are also raised for their soft wool. Vicuñas and guanacos are wild lamoids that roam the mountains. Vicuñas are also sometimes kept as livestock for their wool.

## Giant River Otter

Peruvians call the endangered giant river otter "lobo del río," which means "river wolf." Like wolves, these large, weasel-like animals are predators near the top of the food chain. They can grow up to 6 feet (2 meters) long and weigh 70 pounds (32 kilograms). They hunt fish, snakes, birds, and reptiles.

The giant river otter's long, streamlined body is perfect for fast swimming. It uses its long, flat tail to push through the water. It steers with its webbed feet. The otter's thick fur is nearly waterproof.

Giant river otters once lived throughout South America. Now, only between 2,000 and 5,000 giant river otters are left. In the past, otters were hunted for their fur. Today, it is illegal in Peru and other countries to kill a giant river otter or buy its fur.

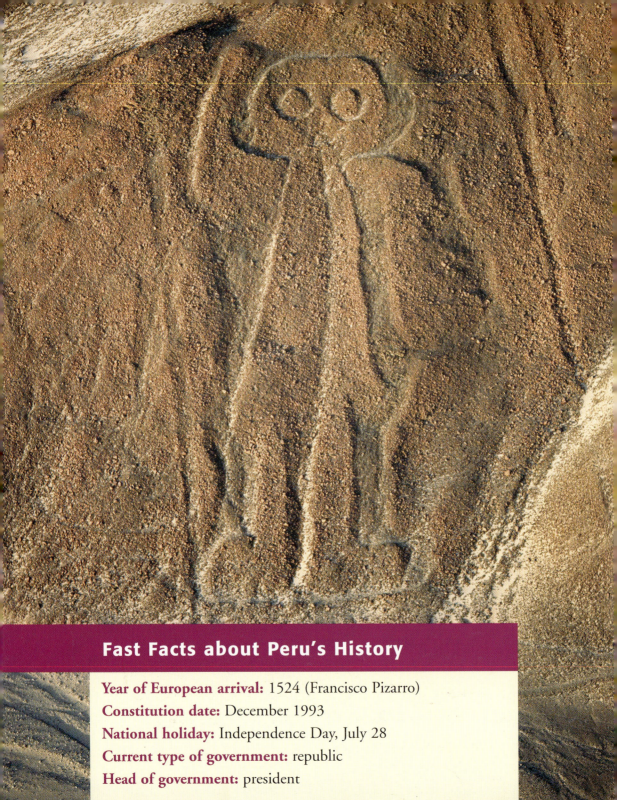

## Fast Facts about Peru's History

**Year of European arrival:** 1524 (Francisco Pizarro)
**Constitution date:** December 1993
**National holiday:** Independence Day, July 28
**Current type of government:** republic
**Head of government:** president

# Chapter 3

# Peru's History and Government

The first people of Peru lived in caves along Peru's coast. Sometime around 2500 B.C., people moved to the fertile areas in the interior of the country. They began growing cotton, beans, squash, peppers, and other crops. Eventually, these groups formed the earliest Peruvian civilizations.

The Chavín civilization was the first known civilization in Peru. The civilization peaked between 800 and 400 B.C. The Chavín introduced weaving into the Peruvian culture. They also created remarkable carvings and statues.

The Nazca culture flourished from 200 B.C. to A.D. 600. The Nazca created the mysterious Nazca lines in the Peruvian deserts. These lines, carved into the desert rock, depict huge animals and geometric shapes. No one is certain about what the animals and the lines mean.

◀ The Nazca culture carved drawings like this one, nicknamed the "astronaut," in Peru's desert.

Around 200 B.C., the Huari and Tiahuanaco cultures developed. The Tiahuanaco, sometimes spelled Tiwanaku, lived near Lake Titicaca. They created large pyramids, temples, and palaces. The Huari, sometimes spelled Wari, lived north of the Tiahuanaco in the Peruvian Andes. The Huari civilization broke up around A.D. 800, while the Tiahuanaco broke up after A.D. 1000. Scientists are unsure why. Many archaeologists believe the Tiahuanaco and Huari greatly influenced the Inca.

## Rise of the Inca

The Inca civilization is Peru's most famous culture. Between about 1200 and 1535, the Inca created an empire that stretched from the equator to Chile. It is unclear how the Inca rose to power, because they left no written records of their history. People learn about them from the buildings, pottery, and other items they left behind. The Spanish also wrote about the Inca when they arrived in Peru.

In Inca culture, the high priest was the ruler. The ruler was called "Inca." Europeans later referred to the entire civilization as the Inca civilization. The Inca ruler was believed to be a descendant of Inti, the Sun god. Inti was the most powerful Inca god. The Inca ruler led the military and all religious ceremonies.

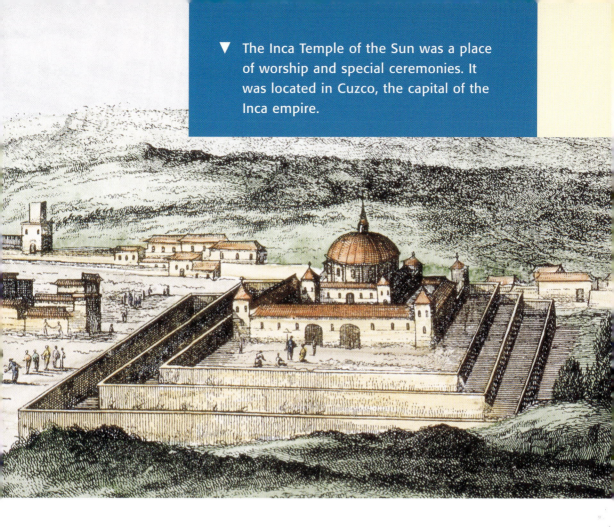

▼ The Inca Temple of the Sun was a place of worship and special ceremonies. It was located in Cuzco, the capital of the Inca empire.

Inca people honored their gods and goddesses, such as the earth and the sea, in ceremonies. Most of these ceremonies included feasting and dancing. People offered food or other goods to the gods. Rarely, in times of sickness, poor crops, or warfare, an animal or a human was sacrificed to the gods. The Inca also decorated their buildings with gold. They believed gold was the sweat of the Sun god.

> **Did you know...?**
> Cuzco was the center of the Inca civilization. This city was built in the shape of a puma and contained temples covered in solid gold.

## Spanish Conquest

In 1524, Spanish explorer Francisco Pizarro came upon Inca cities in his search for gold and treasure in South America. When he saw the Inca's gold treasures, he wanted the gold for himself.

In 1531, he returned with many men to defeat the Inca and take their treasure. Pizarro had lucky timing. The Inca had just fought a civil war. The Inca armies were exhausted and unable to defend the empire. Pizarro and his men easily defeated the Inca armies.

Pizarro then captured the Inca leader Atahualpa and demanded gold for his safe return. The Inca gave Pizarro the gold, but he killed Atahualpa anyway. Without Atahualpa, the Inca had no leader to plan their defense.

Over the next few years, the Spanish gradually took over Inca land. In 1533, Pizarro captured the royal Inca city of Cuzco. In 1535, he founded Lima along the coast. In 1536, the new Inca ruler fled to the remote Peruvian rain forests and built a small city there called Vilcabamba. By 1542, the Spanish had control of the rest of the Inca empire. In 1572, the Spanish captured and killed the last Inca ruler, Tupac Amaru, at Vilcabamba. The once-glorious Inca empire was gone.

▼ Pizarro and his men killed Inca leader Atahualpa, even after the Inca paid for his release.

The Spanish forced thousands of Inca people to mine gold and silver or farm on huge estates. For years, the Spanish sent Peruvian gold and silver to Spain. Peru became the main source of wealth and power for the Spanish empire. Many settlers from Spain came to Peru to make money in the new land.

## Battle for Independence

In the 1700s, Spanish colonists and native people became increasingly unhappy with Spanish rule. Several rebellions took place during the mid-1700s. One of the largest was started by José Gabriel Condorcanqui in 1780. He took the name of Tupac Amaru II because he was related to the last Inca ruler. In 1781, the Spanish government killed Amaru II.

Successful fights for independence did not come until the 1820s. In 1821, José de San Martín of Argentina led an army from the south to free Peru from Spain. San Martín had already led a successful revolt in Chile. He defeated Spanish colonial forces in Lima and other parts of the country and declared Peru independent from Spain. Still, the Spanish held many areas of Peru and did not recognize Peru's independence. In 1824, Simón Bolívar of Venezuela led another independence army from the north into Spanish-controlled areas in Peru. The remaining

▲ Simón Bolívar led an army to finish freeing Peru from Spanish rule.

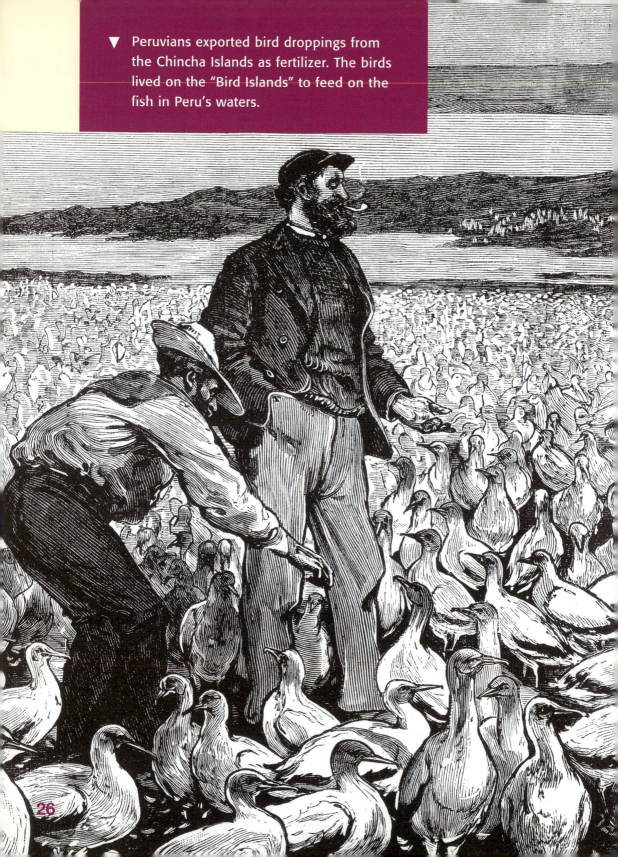

▼ Peruvians exported bird droppings from the Chincha Islands as fertilizer. The birds lived on the "Bird Islands" to feed on the fish in Peru's waters.

Spanish forces were defeated in December 1824. Although Spain did not officially recognize Peru's independence, Spain no longer ruled there.

## The Guano Boom and More Conflict

In the 1840s, Peru began to sell bird droppings from the Chincha Islands. Often called the "Bird Islands," the Chincha Islands are home to millions of birds. Bird droppings were several feet deep on many of the islands. Farmers around the world wanted this guano because it made an excellent fertilizer. Many Peruvians grew rich as a result of this "Guano Boom."

Beginning in the 1860s, Peru battled other countries over territory. Spain tried to take back control of Peru in 1864 in a war that lasted until 1871. Spain finally recognized Peru's independence in 1879. Peru then fought alongside Bolivia against Chile in the War of the Pacific (1879–1883). Peru lost land to Chile during this war.

While the Guano Boom did help the economy, the lives of most people did not improve. Income gaps between the rich and poor grew wider. Leaders spent little time or effort on the problems of hunger, poverty, and joblessness. These social problems kept Peru from developing a strong economy. By the end of the 1800s, Peru was again caught in civil wars and political instability.

## Politics in the 1900s

During the late 1800s and early 1900s, many of Peru's government leaders were military officials. They concentrated on bringing jobs and money to Peru. But many of them ran the government as dictators rather than working with elected legislatures.

Peru's economy grew during the early 1900s. Peru suffered less than other countries through the Great Depression (1929–1939) because its various exports brought money into the country. After World War II (1939–1945), many businesses came to Peru.

In 1963, Fernando Belaúnde was elected president. He introduced economic reforms, education policies, and public works designed to help the poor. In 1968, Belaúnde's government was overthrown by the military, led by General Juan Velasco Alvarado. Alvarado, in turn, was overthrown by General Francisco Morales Bermúdez in 1975.

Although both Alvarado and Bermúdez tried to establish more economic and social reforms, the people grew resentful of military rule. Free democratic elections were restored in 1980. The people elected Belaúnde in this election, sending a clear signal that Peruvians rejected military rule.

▲ Women peel bananas in a food processing plant in Peru in the 1950s. Peru's economy grew greatly after World War II.

▲ The Shining Path guerrilla group used violence to try to achieve their goals.

## Guerrilla Groups and Cocaine

In the 1980s, militant political organizations, called guerrilla groups, began to challenge and threaten the elected government. Members of these groups were unhappy with economic and political conditions. They wanted a socialist government, headed by their leaders. Socialism stresses public ownership of industries. Socialism also stresses help for the poor, with the goal of meeting everyone's basic needs.

Two of the largest guerrilla groups were the Shining Path and the Tupac Amaru Revolutionary Movement (MRTA). These groups used violence to achieve their goals. Sometimes, these groups bombed locations in big cities or attacked government armies. These and other groups fought one another and the government, causing ongoing uncertainty and unrest in the country.

During the 1980s, the demand for the illegal drug cocaine grew. Cocaine is made from the coca plant. Some Peruvians had grown small amounts of coca for medicinal purposes. But as the demand for cocaine grew, more farmers began to grow coca. Coca brings farmers far more money than other traditional Peruvian crops, such as coffee. People who made and sold the illegal drugs became rich and powerful. These drug traffickers often gave money to guerrilla groups.

## Fujimori

In 1990, Alberto Fujimori was elected president. He worked to stop cocaine production and to defeat guerrilla groups. Many leaders of the Shining Path and the MRTA were captured in 1992. Fujimori launched an attack against illegal drugs. The United States worked with Peru's government to stop drug making. By 1999, drug trafficking had decreased by 66 percent.

In 1992, President Fujimori angered many people when he dissolved the legislature. Many thought he was trying to become a dictator. Under pressure, Fujimori held elections for a new legislature in 1992. He also won approval for a new constitution in 1993. This constitution returned Peru to a democratic government. Fujimori promised to honor the new constitution. He was reelected in 1995 and 2000.

## Peru Today

Many groups believed Fujimori won the 2000 election by cheating. After a few months, Fujimori resigned from the presidency. He left Peru to live in Japan. In 2001, new elections were held. Alejandro Toledo became president.

In recent years, Peru's struggle with coca production has continued to be a problem. Colombia and other drug-producing countries have decreased coca production. But demand for cocaine remains strong. The value of coca continues to be higher than the value of legal crops. Some Peruvian farmers are returning to coca farming.

▲ A Peru farm family works in their coca field in 2002.

In 2002, farmers marched against the Peruvian government, demanding that they be allowed to grow whatever crops they chose. In response, the Peruvian government stopped destroying coca crops. The government continues to review its policies on how to effectively stop the drug trade.

## Peru's Government

Peru is a republic with executive, legislative, and judicial branches. All Peruvian citizens age 18 and older are required to vote. They can be fined if they do not vote.

Three members of Peru's executive branch are elected by the people. They are the president, first vice president, and second vice president. The president leads the executive branch. The president is elected for a five-year term and can serve two terms. The president appoints a council of 16 ministers to advise him. One minister is the president of the Council of Ministers. Fifteen other ministers represent agriculture, finance, defense, and other areas of government. The executive branch proposes laws and discusses government policies.

Peru's legislative branch, Congress, is made up of 120 members. They are elected by a popular vote for a five-year term. Members of Congress pass laws, approve treaties, and approve the government budget.

Peru's judicial branch is led by a 16-member Supreme Court. It makes final decisions on court cases appealed from superior courts. Superior courts review the decisions handed up from lower courts. A Constitutional Tribunal interprets civil rights laws.

Peru is subdivided into 24 departments and the district of Callao. Each department is subdivided into

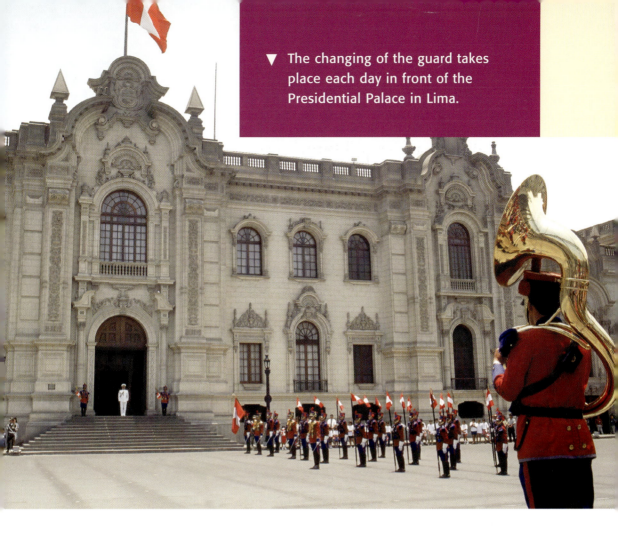

▼ The changing of the guard takes place each day in front of the Presidential Palace in Lima.

districts. Peru's smaller villages and settlements follow a complex system of local government. Some towns have an elected mayor and council. Others have a system known as "indirect rule." Under this system, several small villages are governed by a local priest. The priest's main responsibility is to plan the yearly religious festivals and ceremonies. This leader also performs marriages and serves as judge in moral or religious disputes.

## Fast Facts about Peru's Economy

**Major natural resources:** copper, silver, gold, iron, oil
**Major agricultural products:** cotton, sugar, coffee, rice, potatoes
**Major manufactured products:** cement, textiles, processed fish
**Major imports:** food, machinery, metals, chemicals
**Major exports:** fish meal, cotton, sugar, coffee, minerals

# Chapter 4

# Peru's Economy

Peru has a workforce of about 10 million people. About 10 percent work in agriculture. Most farmers grow coffee, cotton, and food products. Coca is also grown in large quantities, but information on exactly how many Peruvians grow the crop is limited. Commerce and manufacturing employ another 35 percent. The remaining 55 percent of Peruvians work in government, education, and other services.

While Peru's official unemployment rate is 9 percent, many people work in jobs not counted by the government. These workers cannot afford to register as businesses and pay the required taxes. They include street vendors, some bus drivers, and other service providers. These people are considered the informal economy. In the 1980s, it was estimated that 38 percent of all goods and services produced in Peru came from the informal economy.

◀ Street markets are part of Peru's informal economy.

## Agriculture and Fishing

Peru's land and climate influence agriculture. Farmers in the dry coastal region must use irrigation and modern methods and equipment to produce cotton, sugarcane, coffee, wheat, rice, corn, and barley. Farmers also grow crops for their own use, including potatoes, sweet potatoes, vegetables, and fruits.

In the mountains, farmers plant smaller amounts of crops. They often grow only enough food to feed their families and trade locally. They farm using simple tools and methods passed down from their ancestors. They build terraces on the mountain slopes to create flat areas where they can plant crops. These farmers grow potatoes, wheat, corn, and a type of grain called quinoa.

Throughout Peru, many farmers raise cattle, poultry, sheep, llamas, and alpacas. Livestock ranches are found mainly in the mountain valleys. Alpaca wool is one of Peru's most important livestock products. People throughout the world value the soft alpaca wool sweaters, blankets, and other items.

Commercial fishing is another major industry in Peru. Fishers catch anchovies, tuna, and other fish in Peru's waters. Shrimp and other shellfish are also caught in Peru. Peruvians process much of the fish into fish meal. People use fish meal to feed animals and to fertilize crops.

▼ Peru has a large commercial fishing industry.

## Peru's Industries and Natural Resources

**KEY**

- C copper
- cotton
- fish
- gold
- livestock
- manufacturing
- oil
- rice
- silver
- Z zinc

40

In the 1960s, Peruvian fishers took in more than 9 million tons (8 million metric tons) of fish each year. But overfishing and climate changes led to the collapse of the fishing industry in the late 1970s. Today, Peru tries to control overfishing. Limits are placed on the amount of fish people can catch each year. Weather patterns continue to affect the fish industry. In 1993 and 1998, the warm waters of El Niño drove fish away from Peruvian waters, making fish catches less than normal.

> **Did you know...?**
> The United States is the largest buyer of Peru's exports.

## Manufacturing and Mining

Peru continues to diversify its manufacturing industry. Food processing has become one of Peru's largest industries. Food factories produce oils, crackers, bread, cheese, canned foods, and beverages. Textile factories produce clothing for sale within the country and for export. Iron and steel factories make wire and pipe.

Mining has been an important part of Peru's export economy for more than 350 years. Today, modern mining techniques and improved transportation have allowed Peruvians to use their natural resources. Mining is one of the country's fastest-growing industries. Peru is one of the leading producers of gold in South

America. Other valuable metals mined in Peru include zinc, lead, silver, iron, and copper.

In recent years, Peru has become a large oil exporter. The country's main land-based oil fields are found in the northern rain forests. Experts believe huge untapped oil reserves lie off Peru's coast as well.

## Tourism

From the rugged Andes Mountains to the dark Amazon rain forests, Peru has always been an exciting travel spot. Visitors to Peru enjoy some of the world's richest archaeological sites. Inca ruins, including Machu Picchu, are especially popular. Tourists also visit the mysterious Nazca lines. People interested in the rain forest can take eco-tours in Peru. Eco-tours allow visitors to see the rain forest without disturbing wildlife or native people.

In the 1980s and early 1990s, political unrest, guerrilla conflicts, and the illegal drug trade kept many travelers away. Today, Peru's travel and tourism industry is growing because of a more stable economy and government.

## Peru's Money

Peru's official currency is the nuevo sol. The nuevo sol is divided into 100 céntimos. Exchange rates can change every day. In early 2003, 1 U.S. dollar equaled 3.6 nuevos soles and 1 Canadian dollar equaled 2.28 nuevos soles.

5 céntimo coin

50 céntimo coin

10 céntimo coin

20 nuevo sol bill

1 céntimo coin

1 sol coin

20 céntimo coin

10 nuevo sol bill

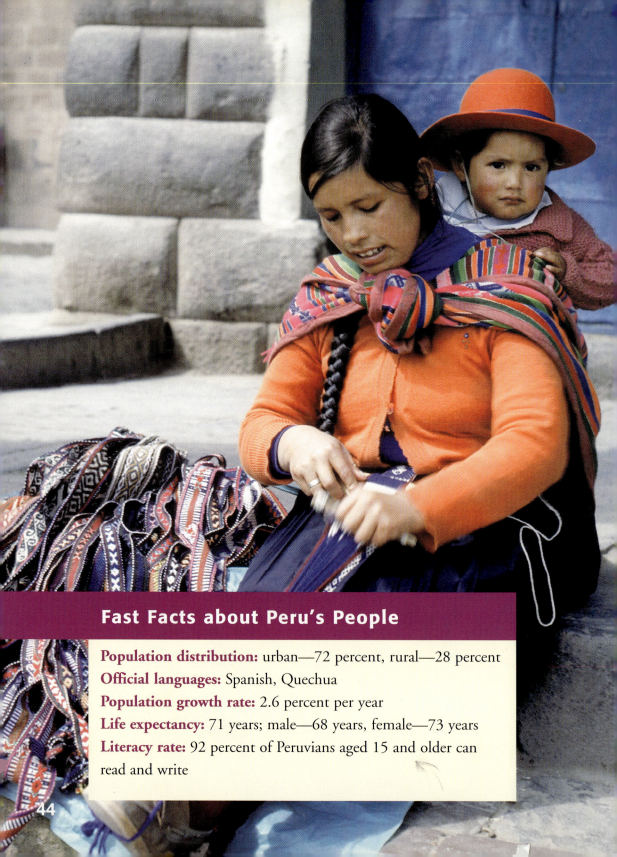

## Fast Facts about Peru's People

**Population distribution:** urban—72 percent, rural—28 percent
**Official languages:** Spanish, Quechua
**Population growth rate:** 2.6 percent per year
**Life expectancy:** 71 years; male—68 years, female—73 years
**Literacy rate:** 92 percent of Peruvians aged 15 and older can read and write

Chapter 5

# Peru's People, Culture, and Daily Life

Peru's population has exploded over the last 60 years. In 1940, only about 7 million people lived in the country. In 2002, Peru's population was almost 28 million.

## Ethnic Groups and Class

Peru struggles with a wide economic and social gap between classes. Before the first Spanish explorers arrived in Peru, the Inca were the most powerful Peruvians. When the Spanish conquered the country, Spanish language and culture became the language and culture of the ruling class.

Generally, the Spanish and their descendants maintained control of government and became wealthy. The native peoples were forced to become slaves and servants or take low-paying jobs. They became the lower class.

◀ A Quechua woman weaves cloth. Peru is known for its bright, woven textiles.

▼ The Aymara live near Lake Titicaca. They use the reeds to make boats, although the practice is less common than in the past.

Later, some Spanish colonists and native people intermarried. Their children became known as mestizo. Mestizo means a person with Spanish and native Indian ancestors. Currently, about 37 percent of Peruvians consider themselves mestizo.

About 45 percent of Peru's people are native Indians. The largest group is the Quechua, who are descendants of the Inca. Most Quechua live in the sierra and high selva areas of Peru. Their language is an official language of Peru. Another group, the Aymara, live mainly around Lake Titicaca in southern Peru. Some native people live in the rain forest.

Today, people of solely European descent make up only a small part of Peru's population. Until the 1960s, they controlled most of Peru's government and industries. A series of reforms in the 1960s took away some of their power and landholdings.

Today, most power still remains with Peruvians of European descent. Native peoples experience housing and job discrimination. The government has passed laws to protect natives from discrimination, but some people still do not accept or treat them as equals.

## Religion

The Spanish brought Roman Catholicism to Peru when they arrived in the 1500s. Roman Catholicism was Peru's official religion until 1979. In that year, the government decided to have no official religion.

Today, more than 90 percent of Peru's people are Roman Catholic. In some areas of the country, people practice a faith that mixes Christian and traditional native beliefs. In some rural areas, people still follow traditional religions.

## Housing

Housing in Peru, and throughout the world, depends on people's wealth. Wealthy families live in large, modern homes. The poor live in city slums and in small villages in the country.

Almost half of Peru's poor city dwellers live on public land in squatter settlements called "pueblos jovenes," or young towns. Squatters live on land illegally.

When people first move to a pueblo joven, they build homes out of scavenged material. In time, some save enough money to build brick homes in place of their makeshift homes. The government has given up trying to force people to move from some pueblos jovenes. The government has added electricity, water, and sewage systems to these young towns.

Native peoples of the Andes live in a variety of homes. The Quechua live in small villages in the Andes. Most build their own one-room houses with mud walls and straw roofs. The Aymara used to build their houses and boats with reeds that grow around Lake Titicaca. Today, most Aymara live in stone or hardened mud homes and use wooden or aluminum boats. The Uros live on large reed rafts on Lake Titicaca. The rafts are often called "floating islands."

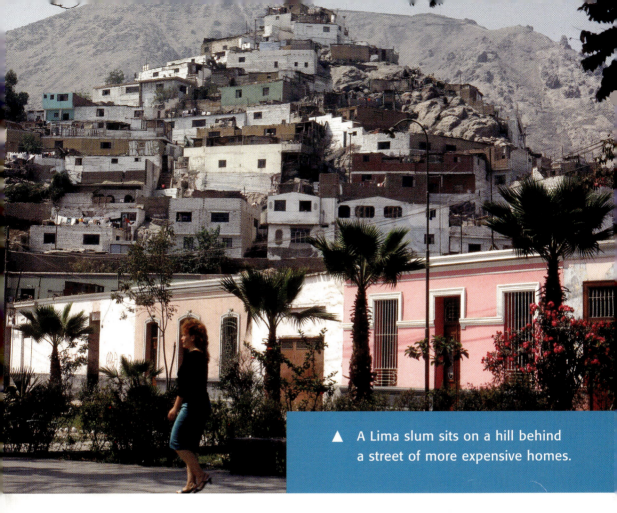

▲ A Lima slum sits on a hill behind a street of more expensive homes.

Villagers in the rain forest might make bamboo houses. Rain forest villages are usually located near a river for water and transportation.

## Education

Peru's government provides free education for children. About 84 percent of Peru's students attend public schools. Other children attend private schools.

# Learn to Speak Spanish

Peruvians have two official languages, Spanish and Quechua. Most Peruvians speak Spanish. Some helpful Spanish words appear below.

**hello**—hola (OH-lah)
**good-bye**—adios (ah-dee-OHS)
**yes**—sí (SEE)
**no**—no (NOH)
**friend**—amigo (ah-MEE-goh)
**thank you**—gracias (GRAH-see-ahs)
**Where is the bathroom?**—
¿Dónde está el baño?
(DON-deh ess-TAH el BAHN-yoh)

▲ Children in Peru learn to read and write Spanish in school.

Although education is free, many children do not attend public school. Some children in rural areas must help their families with chores. Some simply live too far from the nearest school to attend. Many families cannot afford school supplies. A lack of teachers and resources also keeps children away from school. Still, Peruvians believe education is important. Peru has an excellent literacy rate. About 92 percent of Peruvians older than age 15 can read and write.

## Clothing and Food

Clothing in Peru differs by ethnic group and location. Most urban Peruvians wear clothing similar to clothing worn in the United States and Europe. Rural native people often wear traditional dress. Men typically wear a chullo, which is a llama wool hat that covers the ears. They also wear a poncho over a white shirt. They make sandals called ojotas. Women usually wear blouses and long, wide skirts. Women in different cities wear different types of hats. A woman's hat can show where she lives.

Peruvian food also differs by location. People along the coast enjoy a wide variety of seafood. Ceviche is a popular, marinated raw fish dish with onions, peppers, and potatoes or corn. Farmers in the Andes grow more than 200 varieties of potatoes.

> **Did you know...?**
> Potatoes originally came from Peru.

Stews with potatoes and dried meats are popular. Some Andes dwellers eat the native guinea pig, called cuy, on special occasions. People in the rain forest often have the most varied diet. The forest holds many types of fruits, nuts, and wild animals. People catch fish in the rivers. Cassava is a staple food for many native peoples. Cassava is a root often made into tapioca.

Although the coca plant can be turned into the illegal drug cocaine, coca has a variety of legal uses. Local people chew coca leaves or brew them into a tea to use as a medicine to relieve sickness and pain.

## Sports, Arts, and Leisure

Peruvians enjoy a wide variety of sports. Many people climb mountains in the Andes region. Coastal waters offer swimming, boating, skiing, and surfing. Soccer, tennis, golf, and fencing are also popular. Many Peruvians also enjoy watching bullfights. Bullfights may be between a person and a bull, or between two bulls.

Peru's native people are known throughout the world for their handicrafts. One of their most important craft skills is weaving. Peruvian weaving includes bright, bold patterns related to a specific village or a time in history. Weavers use soft alpaca wool to create rugs, clothing, and other items.

# Make Arroz Con Leche

Rice pudding is a popular dish throughout Peru. Traditional rice pudding is not very thick. Ask an adult to help you with this recipe.

## What You Need

### Ingredients
1 cup (240 mL) rice
4 cups (960 mL) milk
1 cup (240 mL) sugar
cinnamon sticks

### Equipment
large saucepan with lid
liquid-ingredient measuring cup
dry-ingredient measuring cup
large spoon
pot holders

## What You Do

1. Put rice, milk, sugar and 1 cinnamon stick in a large saucepan and cover.
2. Cook over medium heat for 15 minutes, stirring often.
3. Remove cover and increase temperature until the mixture is gently boiling. Continue cooking for 30 minutes, stirring often so mixture does not stick to saucepan. It is especially important to stir constantly near the end of the cooking time.
4. When the milk has thickened, but not to typical pudding texture, remove from heat with pot holders.
5. Remove cinnamon stick. Serve warm, or cool in refrigerator and serve cold.

Makes 4 to 6 servings

Music from the Andes region uses a wide variety of instruments. Skilled musicians play harps, violins, small guitars, native flutes, and panpipes. This mix of instruments creates unique dance music.

## Holidays and Celebrations

Many Peruvian holidays are based on religion. Christians celebrate Easter and the week before Lent, called Carnaval. They also celebrate the Immaculate Conception on December 8 and Christmas on December 25. Many cities celebrate their patron Christian saints. El Señor de los Milagros (Lord of the Miracles) takes place in October. It honors the patron saint of Lima. It ends with a huge procession where people carry an image of the saint. In Cuzco on June 24, the large celebration of Inti Raymi, Festival of the Sun, honors the Inca Sun god.

An important holiday is Independence Day on July 28. Most people have two days off work during this holiday. The president usually gives a speech to the nation. A parade is held with military personnel, schoolchildren, and politicians. Families spend the holiday having fun together.

Despite previous political unrest, Peruvians are proud of their country. The economy continues to grow and heritage remains important. Peruvians look forward to a bright future.

◄ People in elaborate costumes wait to begin a parade for the Virgen del Carmen Christian holiday in Paucartambo.

▲ The cock-of-the-rock is Peru's national bird.

# Peru's National Symbols

### ◀ Peru's Flag
The Peruvian flag was created in 1820. It has two vertical red bars with a white bar down the center. Peru's coat of arms lies in the center of the white bar. Legend says that the colors of the flag came from General José de San Martín during the war to liberate Peru from Spanish rule. He was supposedly inspired as he watched flamingos with red wings and white breasts fly overhead.

### ◀ Peru's Coat of Arms
The Peruvian coat of arms was made official in 1825. An oak crown tops the design. The arms show a vicuña in the upper left and a cinchona tree in the upper right. Quinine is extracted from this tree to make a treatment for the disease malaria. A golden cornucopia, or horn of plenty, spills out coins on the bottom of the shield. These symbols represent Peru's animal, vegetable, and mineral wealth.

### Other National Symbols
**National anthem:** Marcha Nacional (National March)
**National flower:** kantuta
**National tree:** cinchona
**National bird:** cock-of-the-rock

# Timeline

**200 B.C.**
The Nazca, Huari, and Tiahuanaco civilizations develop. Of these, the Tiahaunaco lasts the longest, until A.D. 1000.

**1524**
Francisco Pizarro first encounters the Inca.

**1821**
José de San Martín declares Peru independent of Spain.

**1824**
Simón Bolívar frees additional areas of Peru.

B.C.　　A.D.　　1500　　　　1800

**800 BC**
The Chavín civilization develops.

**A.D. 1200**
The Inca civilization begins to rule most of Peru.

**1572**
The Spanish kill the last Inca ruler, Tupac Amaru.

**1879**
Spain recognizes Peru's independence.

Peru and Bolivia battle Chile in the War of the Pacific.

**1929–1939**
The Great Depression affects economies around the world.

**1968**
General Velasco Alvarado overthrows Belaúnde's government.

**1980**
Free elections are restored in Peru.

**2002**
Peru suspends destruction of coca farms due to mass protests by coca farmers.

**1900** — **2000**

**1963**
Fernando Belaúnde is elected president.

**1975**
Velasco Alvarado is overthrown by Francisco Morales Bermúdez.

**1993**
Peru's current constitution is approved.

# Words to Know

**alpaca** (al-PAK-uh)—a domesticated mammal of the camel family known for its beautiful wool

**cocaine** (koh-KAYN)—an illegal drug made from the coca plant

**commerce** (KOM-urss)—the buying and selling of things in order to make money

**corruption** (kuh-RUPHT-shuhn)—dishonest behavior

**dictator** (DIK-tay-tur)—someone who has complete control of a country, often ruling it unjustly

**drug trafficking** (DRUG TRAF-ick-ing)—the importing and exporting of illegal drugs

**guano** (GWAH-noh)—animal droppings

**guerrilla group** (guh-RIL-uh GROOP)—a group that seeks to radically change the government, often using violence

**pueblo joven** (PWEB-loh HO-ven)—an illegally occupied settlement, Spanish for "young town"

**quinoa** (KEEN-oh-uh)—a type of plant grown in the Andes whose seeds are often ground and eaten

**sacrifice** (SAK-ruh-fisse)—to offer something to a god

**scavenged** (SKAV-uhngd)—materials that have been thrown away, for which others find use

# To Learn More

**Corona, Laurel.** *Peru.* Modern Nations of the World. San Diego: Lucent Books, 2001.

**Drew, David.** *Inca Life.* Early Civilizations. Hauppauge, N.Y.: Barron's Educational Series, 2000.

**King, David C.** *Peru: Lost Cities, Found Hopes.* Exploring Cultures of the World. New York: Benchmark Books, 1998.

**Macdonald, Fiona.** *Inca Town.* Metropolis. New York: Franklin Watts, 1998.

**Morrison, Marion.** *Peru.* Enchantment of the World. Second Series. New York: Children's Press, 2000.

**Reinhard, Johan.** *Discovering the Inca Ice Maiden: My Adventures on Ampato.* Washington, D.C.: National Geographic Society, 1998.

# Useful Addresses

**Embassy of Peru in Canada**
130 Albert Street
Suite 1901
Ottawa, ON  K1P 5G4

**Peruvian Embassy in Washington, D.C.**
1700 Massachusetts Avenue NW
Washington, DC  20036

# Internet Sites

**Do you want to learn more about Peru?**
Visit the FactHound at *http://www.facthound.com*

FactHound can track down many sites to help you. All the FactHound sites are hand-selected by our editors. FactHound will fetch the best, most accurate information to answer your questions.

IT'S EASY! IT'S FUN!
1) Go to *http://www.facthound.com*
2) Type in: 0736821767
3) Click on "FETCH IT" and FactHound will put you on the trail of several helpful links.

You can also search by subject or book title. So, relax and let our pal FactHound do the research for you!

▲ Bullfighting is a popular sport in Peru.

# Index

agriculture, 9, 32, 37, 38
alpacas, 16, 38, 52
Amaru, Tupac, 22
Amaru, Tupac II, 24
Andes Mountains, 9, 10, 14, 16, 20, 42, 48, 51
art, 52
Atahualpa, 22, 23
Aymara, 46, 47, 48

Belaúnde, Fernando, 28
Bingham, Hiram, 5
Bolívar, Simón, 24, 25

Chavín civilization, 19
Chile, 6, 20, 24, 27
Chincha Islands, 26, 27
climate, 12–14, 38, 41
clothing, 51
coast, 9–10, 13, 14, 19, 38, 42, 52
coat of arms, 57
coca, 32–33, 52
Condorcanqui, José Gabriel. See Amaru, Tupac II
crafts, 52
Cuzco, 5, 22

drugs, 31, 32–33, 42, 52. See also coca

education, 37, 49, 51
El Niño, 13–14, 41
ethnic groups, 45–47, 48, 51

farming. See agriculture
fishing, 38, 39, 41
flag, 57
fog, 10

food, 37, 38, 41, 51–52, 53
Fujimori, Alberto, 31–32

gold, 21, 22, 24, 41
government
    branches of, 34
    local government, 34–35
Guano Boom, 26, 27
guerrilla groups, 30–31, 42

holidays, 55
housing, 47, 48–49
Huari, 20
Humboldt Current. See Peru Current

Inca, 5–6, 20–21, 22–24, 42, 45
independence from Spain, 24, 27
informal economy, 37
irrigation, 10, 38

Lake Titicaca, 11, 20, 46, 47, 48
Lima, 10, 24, 35, 49, 55

Machu Picchu, 5, 42
manufacturing, 37, 41
military, 28
mining, 41–42
music, 55

natural resources, 6, 40, 41–42
Nazca, 19, 42

Peru Current, 13
Pizarro, Francisco, 22, 23
plant life, 16
population, 6, 45
pueblos jovenes, 48

Quechua, 45, 46–47, 48

rainfall, 14
rain forest, 6, 9, 12, 13, 14, 16, 42, 49
religion, 35, 47, 55
    of the Inca, 20–21

San Martín, José de, 24
Sechura Desert, 9
selva, 12, 13, 14, 47
service industry, 37
Shining Path, 30, 31
sierra, 10–11, 14, 47
socialism, 30–31
Spanish conquest, 22–24, 45
sports, 52

temperature, 13, 14
Tiahuanaco, 20
Toledo, Alejandro, 32
tourism, 6, 42

War of the Pacific, 27
wildlife, 16, 17, 42
workforce, 37